Beyond ABC

Written by Lisa Holt & Lyn Wendon
Illustrated by Doreen Shaw

Based on characters originated by Lyn Wendon.

Welcome back to Letterland

As you may already know, the people and animals in Letterland usually hide behind their plain black letter shapes. Fortunately, in this book you can look into their secret land to see what they are really like. You will also discover some Letterland stories about what happens when these characters come together in words!

Are you ready?
Let's go!

Clever Cat belongs to Harry Hat Man. He looks after her well and she loves him. But she has one problem. As soon as she finds herself next to him in a word, she can't make her usual 'c...' sound because his hairy hat makes her nose tickle. So all you can hear when these two are together is Clever Cat's little sneezing sound, '**ch**...'.

Clever Cat was calmly playing **ch**ess in the kit**ch**en, but then the clock **ch**imed and Harry came hopping in to get his lun**ch**. He was horrified to see **ch**icks and a **ch**icken on a **ch**air, so he's been trying to **ch**ase them out. The trouble is, all that **ch**arging about has made Clever Cat start sneezing "**ch**" again! Let's help Harry **ch**oose his lun**ch** so he can hop off again. There's some **Ch**inese food, some **ch**eese and some **ch**unks of **ch**ocolate. There are some pea**ch**es and a **ch**erry cake, too. Whi**ch** would you **ch**oose for your lun**ch**?

chair   cheese   chicken   chocolate

Harry Hat Man knows that Peter Puppy is sometimes sad because his ears droop. He also knows that Peter Puppy loves having his **ph**otogra**ph** taken. So whenever they sit together in a word Harry takes his **ph**otogra**ph**. Peter Puppy smiles and Harry Hat Man even laughs — quietly though — with his mouth half shut and his teeth on his lips. So his usual 'hhh...' sound becomes a 'fff...' sound, just like Firefighter Fred's sound. Hear it twice in the word **ph**otogra**ph**!

Today Harry is getting some tips from **Ph**illipa, the **ph**otogra**ph**er. She has won tro**ph**ies for her **ph**otos of dol**ph**ins and ele**ph**ants. Can you see them on the wall and on the pam**ph**lets? Look! She's **ph**otogra**ph**ing some **ph**easants. Harry took a **ph**oto of a saxo**ph**one and a sap**ph**ire this morning. Now he's taking another **ph**otogra**ph** of Peter Puppy to make him even happier.

dolphin   elephant   phone   photograph

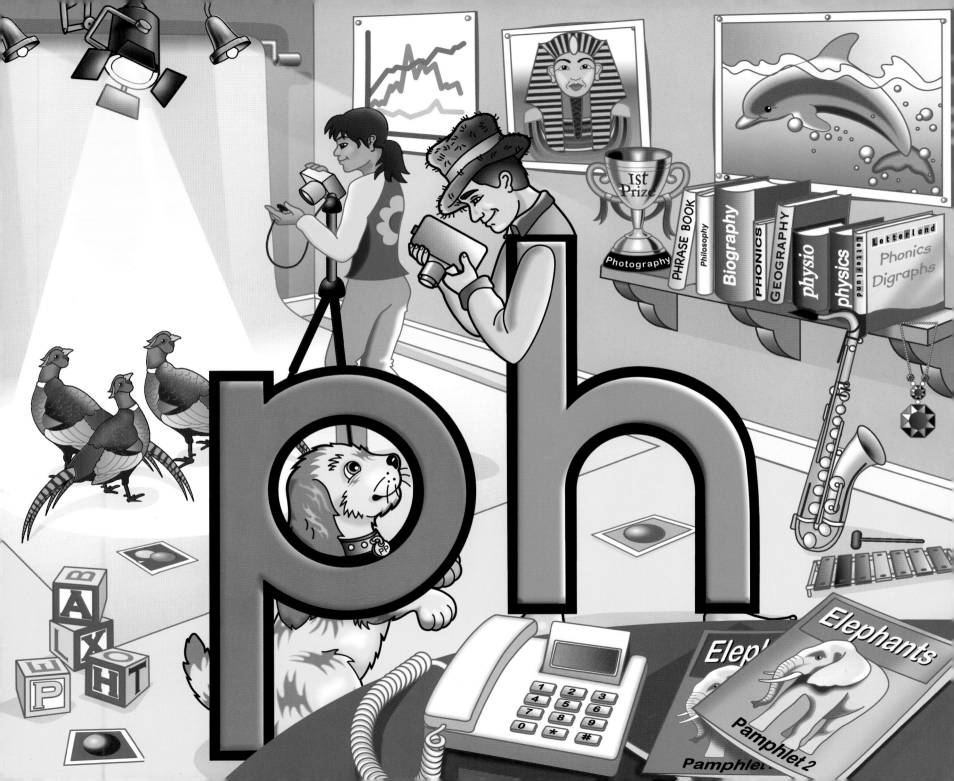

What sound does Sammy usually make in words? Yes, he likes to hiss 'sss...' very loudly. How does Harry Hat Man feel about noise? That's right, he hates it! So what do you think happens when Sammy comes slithering and sliding up behind Harry in a word? Do you think he will put up with all that noise? Absolutely not! He turns back and says "**sh**!" to hu**sh** Sammy up.

Sammy came slithering up behind Harry at the sea**sh**ore today, hissing loudly, so Harry had to say "**sh**!" again. Sammy and Harry like to sit in the sun**sh**ine and look at all the things by the **sh**ore. They can see **sh**ells, **sh**rimps and fi**sh** in the sea. Those fi**sh sh**ould keep a **sh**arp eye out for that **sh**ark in the **sh**allow water!

Can you see the **sh**epherd **sh**earing his **sh**eep? There are four **sh**y **sh**eep who don't want to be **sh**eared. Can you find them for him?

ship   shell   sheep   shark

When Tess and Harry get together in words you'll hear either the unvoiced **th** sound in **th**ink, or the voiced **th** sound, as in **th**ere.

Talking Tess spends a lot of time making her tiny 't…' sound in many words. But have you ever noticed **th**at Tess and Harry Hat Man make a completely different sound when **th**ey're toge**th**er? Talking Tess blames it on the wea**th**er – especially **th**understorms. Talking Tess loves **the th**understorms, but Harry hates **th**em – **th**ey're so loud! So Talking Tess hurries up to Harry to comfort him as she says, "**Th**ere, **th**ere. It's only **the th**under!"

Tess and Harry are hurrying home from **the th**eatre to get away from **the th**under. Nobody else seems bo**th**ered by **the th**under. **The th**rushes are **th**irsty so **th**ey are still in **th**eir bird ba**th**. **The** girl on **the th**rone hasn't put away her **th**imble and **th**read yet, and **the** a**th**lete by **the th**atched cottage is still **th**rowing his javelin. **Th**ankfully, I **th**ink **the th**under won't last more **th**an **th**irty seconds!

there   three   thirty   thunder   thumb

In a few words Harry gets so annoyed at Walter that he shouts, 'Who do you think you are?' and throws a bucket of water at Walter Walrus instead! Now who is too startled to speak? Yes, Walter Walrus!

Walter Walrus hates it when Harry Hat Man gets in his way so that he can't see ahead. Not only is Harry tall, but he also wears a hat, blocking Walter's view even more! So what does Walter do? He whooshes that hat off with a big wave of water! Then poor Harry Hat Man is too startled to speak. That is why we only hear Walter in words like when, which, what, where and why.

Look! Walter has whacked Harry's hat off again, while Harry wasn't looking! Perhaps Walter wants to see what the girl near the wheeled bin is whistling about. It looks like she has spotted a whale in the whirlpool. The man with the white shirt in the wheat field hasn't seen the whale yet. Maybe he's just too busy whittling to notice it. What do you think he might be whittling? Do you think his pet whippet hopes it will be something for him?

who   whale   wheat   wheel   white

Whenever you see Walter Walrus next to Annie Apple in a word, don't expect her to make her usual sound. That's because Walter Walrus is busy teasing her by splashing her with salty water. When he splashes Annie Apple we hear her cry out, "**AW**! Don't be so **aw**ful!"

It's d**aw**n in Letterland but Walter is already up to his tricks, splashing Annie on the l**aw**n while others are still y**aw**ning. Can you see the girl on the sees**aw** wearing a sh**aw**l? The little f**aw**n is watching her y**aw**n while the other f**aw**n is eating some str**aw**. Can you also see the sharp-beaked h**aw**k in the tree above the s**aw**? Do you think the h**aw**k feels like y**aw**ning too?

The cat is getting **aw**fully wet p**aw**s as she cr**aw**ls across the l**aw**n. How many p**aw** prints can you see on the l**aw**n?

dawn   lawn   paw   seesaw

ew

We know Walter Walrus is a trouble-maker. He loves to tease, and Eddy Elephant doesn't like being splashed. So when Eddy finds himself next to Walter Walrus in a word, he always acts first. He uses his trunk to squirt water at Walter instead. Walter is so surprised he cries out, "Oo! You!" That's why, when you see Eddy Elephant and Walter Walrus together in a word, you can be sure to hear an 'ew...'(oo) sound or a 'ew...'(you) sound.

Walter and Eddy are on the deck of a n**ew** ship. A cr**ew** member is busy handing out a f**ew** bags of cash**ew** nuts. There's a lovely vi**ew**, and there's a man intervi**ew**ing a fine lady in j**ew**els for the n**ew**s. The st**ew**ard is bringing them some delicious st**ew** served with n**ew** potatoes. You would think Walter and Eddy would be happy, but oh no, Eddy just bl**ew** some more water at Walter!

crew   jewels   news   view

Whenever you see Walter Walrus next to Oscar Orange in a word, guess what? You can expect trouble! Walter Walrus starts splashing salty water again and it gets in Oscar's eyes. But Walter always forgets that when you tease someone, you can end up hurting yourself too. Walter loses his balance and bumps his chin, so n**ow** they both h**ow**l, "**OW**!"

While Oscar and Walter are both h**ow**ling "**ow**!", the children are having fun chasing each other and playing with the inflatable v**ow**els d**ow**n in the pool. Not everyone is happy, though. Look at the lady fr**ow**ning as she holds up her dressing g**ow**n. Her g**ow**n and the t**ow**els are damp as they were too close to that p**ow**erful sh**ow**er. Can you see the cr**ow**d under the tree near the t**ow**er in the t**ow**n? Do you think they are looking at the c**ow**s? **How** many br**ow**n c**ow**s can you see?

brown   cow   owl   towel

No diving allowed

Talcum Powder

Mr O is an old man. He has been around for such a long time he kn**ow**s almost all there is to kn**ow**! So he kn**ow**s that Walter Walrus likes to tease Oscar Orange by splashing him. That's why whenever he can, he rushes up to protect Oscar in words, crying out, "**O**h no you don't!" In fact old Mr O cries "**O**h!" so loudly that Walter Walrus is too surprised to make any sound at all.

It's a lovely spring day in the mead**ow**. The sn**ow** has melted and the rabbits are busy building new burr**ow**s. A breeze is bl**ow**ing in the will**ow**s and hedger**ow**s. It's a perfect day for playing b**ow**ls and m**ow**ing the lawn. Mr O's cries have scared Walter, but he hasn't scared the cr**ow**s! Look, the farmer is s**ow**ing seeds and a cheeky cr**ow** is foll**ow**ing him. The farmer kn**ow**s that some of his seeds will still gr**ow**. He has already gr**ow**n some fine marr**ow**s for a sh**ow**. Can you see them in his wheel barr**ow**?

arrow   bungalow   window   yellow

I expect you know that both Walter Walrus and Red Robot are trouble-makers in Letterland. So what happens when they meet? Well, Red Robot remembers that Walter causes trouble by splashing water around. But Red Robot doesn't want to get wet. So he quickly captures Walter Walrus in his sack. Then Walter is too shocked to speak! So whenever you see this troublesome pair in a word, expect to hear Red Robot growling 'rrr...' as he rolls along.

Red Robot has **wr**apped the sack around his **wr**ist so Walter can't **wr**iggle out. "What's **wr**ong with that?", Red Robot says to himself. The little **wr**ens are busy **wr**estling with **wr**iggling worms! Nobody has noticed the **wr**ecking ball knocking down the building behind. What a lot of rubbish in the **wr**eckage! There's some **wr**ought iron, a type**wr**iter, some **wr**apping paper and a poster for a **wr**estling match. **Wr**ite down what you can see in the **wr**eckage.

wrapper   wriggle   wrist   wrong

In Letterland, there are five rollerskating robots who cause trouble by capturing vowels even though they know they shouldn't. This one is called **Ar**thur **Ar** and he likes to capture Letterland apples. Look! He is running away with Annie Apple! She is too surprised to make her usual sound. Instead, all you can hear is **Ar**thur **Ar** reporting back to the ringleader, Red Robot, with his last name, "**Ar**!"

Arthur **Ar** waited until it was getting d**ar**k. He thought he could get up to his tricks by the light of the st**ar**s, but now he's stuck trying to escape from a l**ar**ge b**ar**n! The gu**ar**d dog has st**ar**ted b**ar**king to raise the al**ar**m. And now the f**ar**mer has found **Ar**thur's rad**ar** c**ar** p**ar**ked in his y**ar**d. **Ar**thur **Ar** is d**ar**ting around the b**ar**n trying to escape, but there's a guit**ar**, and t**ar**ts, sh**ar**p d**ar**ts and j**ar**s of v**ar**nish in his way. Even a little **ar**madillo is trying h**ar**d to catch **Ar**thur **Ar** and stop him from getting away in his rad**ar** c**ar**!

car farmer garden star

Now you need to learn about **Or**vil **Or**. He's another robot in Letterland who causes trouble by capturing vowels! **Or**vil **Or** likes to run away with oranges. When he is around, don't expect Oscar Orange to make his usual sound. All you can hear is **Or**vil **Or** rep**or**ting back to Red Robot with just one word, his last name, "**Or**!", as he rushes away to his boat by the sh**or**e.

Can you see **Or**vil's boat by the sh**or**e? It looks very st**or**my over there, doesn't it? There's an en**or**mous t**or**nado coming. It's heading for the **or**chard so unf**or**tunately the children playing sp**or**ts will have to run indo**or**s. The st**or**m hasn't stopped **Or**vil **Or** though. As he f**or**ces his way past the h**or**se, it gives a little sn**or**t. But he had better not step on that little p**or**cupine. Can you see it, nibbling away on those ac**or**ns? How do you think **Or**vil will get past that cow with huge h**or**ns?

fork   horse   sport   storm

Now three of the five robots in Letterland are broth**er**s: **Er**nest **Er**, Urgent Ur and Irving Ir. They all make the same sound as they report back to Red Robot, but they capture different vowels. First, let's meet **Er**nest **Er**, the robot who runs away with elephants! When you see **Er**nest **Er** in a word, don't expect to hear Eddy Elephant making his usual sound. All you can hear is **Er**nest **Er** calling out his last name, "**Er**!", as he reports back to Red Robot.

Ernest **Er** is a fast**er** runn**er** than his oth**er** robot broth**er**s. The park rang**er** is c**er**tain he won't be able to catch him as he runs past the beav**er** and the p**er**ch and the ott**er** in the wat**er**. P**er**haps he will al**er**t the helicopt**er** to track down **Er**nest **Er** later. Right now, the rang**er** had bett**er** look aft**er** the badg**er** and the anteat**er** and the flow**er**s and f**er**ns. What oth**er** animals can you see? And who else can you see working in the park?

danger   flower   panther   tiger

WILDLIFE
PARK

DANGER

Herbs

er

This is **Ur**gent **Ur**. You won't see him very often, but when you do he'll be capturing umbrellas. He reports back to Red Robot with just one word, his last name, "**Ur**!" so you can't hear Uppy Umbrella making her usual sound. **Ur**gent **Ur** must have cold feet, because he always t**ur**ns up wearing boots made of thick c**ur**ly p**ur**ple f**ur**. The boots make him a slower runner than his other brothers so you hardly ever see him at the end of words.

What an eventful Th**ur**sday in Letterland! Everyone is talking about it! **Ur**gent **Ur** has jumped off the c**ur**b and smashed an **ur**n. He is dist**ur**bing the t**ur**keys too, though maybe now they'll t**ur**n and see that fox l**ur**king in the bushes. There's a veterinary s**ur**geon's van near the girl who is b**ur**ning leaves. Do you think an animal has been h**ur**t? The cat c**ur**led up by the c**ur**tain doesn't seem to be h**ur**t. Maybe that n**ur**se will be needed to help the man in the h**ur**dle race. He's been h**ur**led right off his horse!

church   fur   nurse   purple

Irving **Ir** is the **thir**d brother in the robot gang. He captures ink, then reports back to Red Robot with his last name, "**Ir**!" so you can't hear Impy Ink making his usual sound. **Ir**ving **Ir** gets into far fewer words than either of his brothers, because most of the ink bottles in Letterland make themselves invisible when they see **Ir**ving **Ir** coming. If Impy Ink gets caught he squ**ir**ts ink on to **Ir**ving's sh**ir**t! That's why v**ir**tually every sh**ir**t **Ir**ving owns is d**ir**ty!

Irving **Ir** has upset the g**ir**l behind him. She has been planning a th**ir**tieth b**ir**thday party for one of the clowns in the c**ir**cus. She has bought him a new sh**ir**t and cooked him some s**ir**loin steak and a b**ir**thday cake too! Now the clown with the hose really needs to squ**ir**t the ink off that brand new sh**ir**t! Do you think **Ir**ving **Ir** has seen the acrobats sw**ir**ling around and the g**ir**l tw**ir**ling her baton? Even the c**ir**cus dog is wh**ir**ling round in c**ir**cles.
Can you find th**ir**teen b**ir**ds here at the c**ir**cus today?

bird   dirt   shirt   skirt

There are five very important men in Letterland — the Vowel Men. You may have already met them. There is Mr A, the Apron Man and Mr E, the Easy Magic Man, Mr I, the Ice Cream Man, Mr O, the Old Man from over the ocean and Mr U, the Uniform Man. The five Vowel Men are the only Letterlanders that ever say their alphabet names in words — A! E! I! O! U!

But what happens when you see these Vowel Men out walking together in Letterland? Most of the time, all you need to do is remember this simple rhyme:

'When two Vowel Men go out walking, the first one does the talking.

The first one says his name, but his friend won't do the same.'

So in a word like **easy**, Mr E says his name "E!", while Mr A stays silent. That is because he is busy looking out for robots who cause trouble by capturing Vowel Men as they walk through Letterland.

Let's join some of the Vowel Men while they are out walking!

Mr A   Mr E   Mr I   Mr O   Mr U

When Mr A and Mr I go out walking, Mr A does the talking.
He just says his name, "**A**!", but his friend won't do the same. He's too busy being the lookout man, on guard against the robots!

Mr A and Mr I are out walking at the r**ai**lway station. They like to watch the tr**ai**ns. They even like w**ai**ting to see tr**ai**ns when it's r**ai**ning! It looks like some r**ai**n and h**ai**l are on the way. I'm afr**ai**d the man who is p**ai**nting the dr**ai**ns will compl**ai**n! But there's a beautiful r**ai**nbow and everyone else looks happy w**ai**ting for their tr**ai**n. There's a girl in a shiny r**ai**ncoat with a lovely d**ai**sy ch**ai**n, a boy m**ai**ling some letters, a s**ai**lor and his friend, and a man reading his d**ai**ly newspaper.

Do you think anyone will go on the Summer Tr**ai**l? They would ride on a tr**ai**n and then go s**ai**ling for a whole day!

paint   rain   sail   train

When Mr E and Mr A go out walking, Mr E usually does the talking. He just says his name, "**E!**", but his friend won't do the same. He's too busy looking out for robots!

Today Mr E and Mr A are out walking in the market. They **ea**ch have a list of things to buy to **ea**t. Can you find them some m**ea**t and some s**ea**food? They would also like h**ea**ps of fruit and vegetables. Can you find them some p**ea**ches, some b**ea**ns, and some p**ea**s? Mr E would like some **tea** and some y**ea**st because he can't resist a ch**ea**p d**ea**l. He has also seen some expensive gl**ea**ming b**ea**ds, but luckily they are not within **ea**sy r**ea**ch!
Mr A is pl**ea**sed as he has spotted a n**ea**t pile of j**ea**ns by that h**ea**p of l**ea**ves. And Mr E is b**ea**ming as he dr**ea**ms about the f**ea**st they will **ea**t when they get home. What a tr**ea**t!

jeans   peas   peaches   tea

When two Mr E's go out walking, the first Mr E does the talking. He just says his name, "**E**!", but his brother won't do the same. He's too busy looking out for robots!

Mr E and his brother are out for a quick walk. It's fr**ee**zing cold, so they n**ee**d to k**ee**p their f**ee**t moving. Behind them, a man is trying to sw**ee**p up the sl**ee**t and snow, but it is just too d**ee**p, and the br**ee**ze makes it difficult for him to s**ee**. It's so icy, the qu**ee**n is exc**ee**ding the sp**ee**d limit coming down the slippery, st**ee**p str**ee**t in her j**ee**p! She likes to come for coff**ee** m**ee**tings here once a w**ee**k. She's also often s**ee**n in the shops, sampling fine ch**ee**ses and buying sw**ee**ts. She loves toff**ee**, but she's never gr**ee**dy and afterwards she always brushes her t**ee**th.

The g**ee**se look happy f**ee**ding on s**ee**ds. They don't seem to mind having fr**ee**zing f**ee**t!

green   street   three   trees

When Mr O and his friend Mr A go out walking, Mr O does the talking. He just says his name, "**O!**", but his friend won't do the same. He's too busy looking out for robots!

Mr O and Mr A are out walking down by the c**oa**st. They stopped at the fl**oa**ting B**oa**ters' Cafe to have a p**oa**ched egg on t**oa**st. Everyone loves to eat p**oa**ched eggs and t**oa**st there – even the g**oa**ts! They get b**oa**t l**oa**ds of l**oa**ves delivered every day to make all the t**oa**st they need! Can you see what is l**oa**ded in the b**oa**t today?

Mr O and Mr A are walking towards the r**oa**d because they can see the Letterland c**oa**ch coming. They often like to travel by c**oa**ch on the r**oa**d along the c**oa**st with its beautiful views. Look out Mr A! Someone has left their socks s**oa**king in a bowl. Don't step on the s**oa**p and get s**oa**ked in the s**oa**py f**oa**m!

boat   coast   goat   toad

How to use this Letterland book

The *Letterland Beyond ABC* is designed for you to share actively with your children. As you read it, they will think of it all as simply fun. But with your help they will also be learning new vocabulary, many important letter combinations (digraphs) and vital listening, speaking and reading skills.

After each story, talk about the Letterland characters and the story reasons for their change of sound. Spend some time finding objects in the illustrations that contain the new sound. Let your listeners point to and speak out the word for each object, so they hear it repeatedly coming from their own mouths. Then re-read the story, all ears listening again for that recurring special sound.

Because every story combined with its illustration, clusters words of a kind, this book can also be a valuable memory aid for spelling. Seek out any missed objects in the lists below. They aren't all mentioned in the stories!

ch	hatch	xylophone	shepherd	path	**wh**	jigsaw	steward
chain	kitchen	trophy	shield	Southport	whale	paw prints	shrew
chair	peaches		shingle	thank you card	wheat	saw	view
chalk		**sh**	ship	thatched	wheateater	seesaw	yew tree
chart	**ph**	bushes	shirt	theatre	wheeled bin	shawl	
checks	alphabet cubes	dish	shoes	Thermos flask	wheel	strawberries	**ow**
cheese	bibliography	fashion	shop	thick	whelk	straws	brown
cherries	digraphs	fish	shore	thimble	whippet	trawler	down
chess	dolphin	mushroom	shorts	thin	whirl	yawn	clown
chest of drawers	elephant	push	shrew	thirsty	whirligig		cows
chicken	graph	radish	shrimp	thirteenth	whiskers		crowd
chick peas	pamphlet	shades	shrub	thirtieth	whisky	**ew**	eyebrow
chicks	pharaoh	shadow	sunshine	thistle	whistle	cashew nuts	flowers
chime	pheasant	shallow	washing	thorns	white	crew	frown
chilli	phone	shapes	wishing well	thread	Whitley Bay	ewe	gown
Chinese food	phonics	shark		three	whittle	flew	howl
chocolate	photographs	shed	**th**	throw		interview	shower
chop	photographer	sheep	athlete	throne	**aw**	jewels	talcum powder
chopsticks	physics	shear	bird bath	throat lozenge	coleslaw	newspaper	town
chunks	sapphire	sheet	birthday card	thrushes	dawn	new potatoes	towel
chutney	saxophone	shell	length	thunder	fawn	preview	tower
handkerchief	sphere	shelves	month	toothbrush	hawk	screws	trowel
						stew	